LIGHTS, CAMERA, ACTION

A YOUNG FILMMAKER'S GUIDE

STEPHEN F. CANINO

NEWMAN SPRINGS PUBLISHING
320 Broad Street
Red Bank, NJ 07701

First originally published by Newman Springs Publishing 2024

ISBN 979-8-89308-605-8 (Paperback)
ISBN 979-8-89308-606-5 (Hardcover)
ISBN 979-8-89308-607-2 (Digital)

Printed in the United States of America

Contents

Introduction

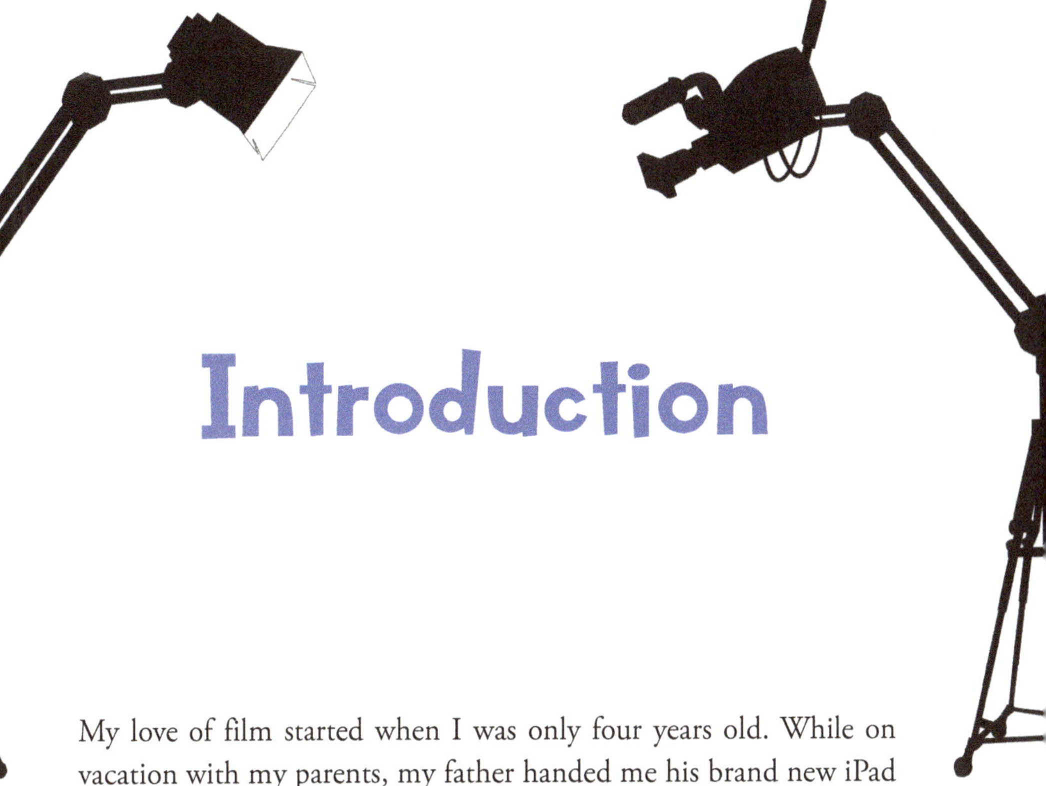

My love of film started when I was only four years old. While on vacation with my parents, my father handed me his brand new iPad to keep me quiet and occupied. He had installed several games for me to play, and those kept me interested—until I discovered the camera feature. That little camera icon at the bottom of the screen would change my life in ways I could not imagine.

My father's belief that handing me his iPad would buy him some peace and quiet proved more incorrect than he could have imagined. He and my mother spent the remainder of that trip following me around while I took photos of everything imaginable. Trees, birds, people, bugs, cars—all were fair game as subjects of my newfound hobby and love.

Every birthday and holiday gift request from that point forward, to this day, was a camera of some kind. At first I was given an inexpensive pocket-sized digital camera. Then a waterproof digital camera which had me sticking my head in the bathtub more times than I can imagine, and then, finally, the holy grail: a Canon DSLR camera with an 8GB SD card (keep in mind, this was many years ago).

Everything changed again as I began to explore my new camera; it even had a video function! From that point forward, cinematography would consume my life. I set up a green screen in the basement of our home, rigged my own makeshift set lights, and embarked upon my young career as a filmmaker. Nearly a decade later, I got a job in a local restaurant (a job I still have to this day) so that I could earn enough money to continuously "feed" my hobby, subsequently buying steadicams/stabilizers, video editing software, professional lighting and the like. Because I was fortunate enough to have grown up in New York City, I would spend weekends browsing the mecca of video equipment, B&H Electronics. I even took extensive work as an extra on numerous TV shows and films, an opportunity for me to not only earn extra money (to buy more film equipment) but also for me to witness firsthand the actual workings of professional film directors and their crew.

While other kids were playing basketball or soccer, I was making films. I devoted myself during 7th and 8th grade to being the school's official "documentarian." I would record everything from sports to theatrical productions. I was then accepted into the visual arts/film program at my local high school, where I continued to produce numerous films. My plans are to continue with my film career and couple it with business studies at college. In the meanwhile, I felt that I had to share my thoughts, tips and tricks with other young adults who have similarly been bitten by the cinematography bug.

Chapter 1

The History and Importance of Filmmaking: A Comprehensive Overview

Filmmaking stands as one of the most influential and cherished art forms of modern times, captivating audiences across the globe with its ability to entertain, educate, and provoke thought. Its rich history is marked by innovation, creativity, and cultural significance, making it an integral part of our collective human experience.

The Origins of Filmmaking: The journey of filmmaking began long before the invention of the modern motion picture camera. From ancient cave paintings depicting stories of hunting and daily life to the innovative shadow plays of ancient China and Greece, humans have always possessed a desire to capture and share narratives visually.

The 19th Century: The true birth of filmmaking can be traced back to the 19th century, with the invention of photographic devices such as the camera obscura and the zoetrope. These early inventions laid the groundwork for the development of motion picture technology, paving the way for the creation of the first moving images.

In 1895, the Lumière brothers, Auguste and Louis, held the first public screening of moving pictures in Paris, France, marking the official birth of cinema. Their short films, including iconic titles like *Arrival of a Train at La Ciotat* and *Workers Leaving the Lumière Factory*, captured the imagination of audiences and set the stage for the rapid evolution of filmmaking as an art form.

The Silent Era: The early years of cinema, known as the silent era, saw filmmakers experimenting with storytelling techniques and visual aesthetics. Lacking the ability to sync audio to moving images, the creative minds behind these silent films relied on intertitles and expressive performances to convey narrative, showcasing the power of visual storytelling in its purest form.

During this time, pioneering filmmakers such as D.W. Griffith, Charlie Chaplin, and Sergei Eisenstein pushed the boundaries of cinematic language, introducing innovative editing techniques, elaborate set designs, and groundbreaking special effects.

The Golden Age of Hollywood: The advent of sound technology in the late 1920s revolutionized the film industry, ushering in the Golden Age of Hollywood. Iconic films like *The Jazz Singer* and *Lights of New York* were among the first films to incorporate synchronized sound for dialogue. These immersive soundscapes captured audiences, and made the experience of viewing film even more lifelike.

Throughout the 1930s and 1940s, Hollywood became the epicenter of global filmmaking, producing an abundance of classic films and iconic stars that continue to resonate with audiences to this day. The studio system, characterized by vertically integrated production companies like MGM, Warner Bros., and Paramount Pictures, dominated the industry and shaped the landscape of popular cinema.

The Rise of World Cinema: While Hollywood remained a dominant force in the global film industry, filmmakers from around the world began to emerge, bringing diverse perspectives and cultural influences to the medium. The rise of world cinema in the mid-20th century gave rise to iconic filmmakers such as Akira Kurosawa, Federico Fellini, and Ingmar Bergman, whose groundbreaking films challenged traditional narrative conventions and pushed the boundaries of cinematic expression.

The New Hollywood Era: The late 1960s and 1970s saw the emergence of the New Hollywood era, characterized by a wave of young, innovative filmmakers who rejected the studio system in favor of creative autonomy and artistic freedom. Directors like Martin Scorsese, Francis Ford Coppola, and Steven Spielberg ushered in a new era of American cinema, producing a diverse range of films that reflected the social, political, and cultural upheavals of the time.

The Digital Revolution: The advent of digital technology in the late 20th century revolutionized the filmmaking process, democratizing access to conventional tools and techniques of production. Digital cameras, non-linear editing systems, and computer-generated imagery (CGI) opened up new possibilities for filmmakers, enabling them to bring their creative visions to life with greater flexibility and efficiency.

The Importance of Filmmaking: Filmmaking holds immense cultural, artistic, and societal importance, serving as a powerful medium for storytelling, self-expression, and social commentary. Through the lens of cinema, filmmakers have the ability to explore complex themes, challenge prevailing ideologies, and shed light on marginalized voices and experiences.

Films have the power to inspire, educate, and provoke change, sparking conversations and fostering empathy across diverse audiences. From Hollywood blockbusters to independent documentaries, each film offers a unique perspective on the world, inviting viewers to engage with new ideas, perspectives, and realities.

Moreover, filmmaking plays a crucial role in preserving cultural heritage and documenting historical events for future generations. Through the preservation and restoration of film archives, filmmakers ensure that our collective memories and experiences are safeguarded for posterity, allowing future generations to learn from the past and gain insight into the human condition.

Concluding, the history and importance of filmmaking are deeply intertwined with the evolution of human society and culture. From its beginnings as a novelty attraction to its current status as a global industry, filmmaking continues to captivate and inspire audiences around the world, reaffirming its status as one of the most cherished and enduring forms of artistic expression.

Why filmmaking is an exciting and accessible art form for young adults:

Filmmaking stands out as an exceptionally exciting and accessible art form for young adults due to its unique blend of creativity, use of technology (where young adults often excel and remain on the cutting edge), and storytelling. In today's digital age, young adults are not only avid consumers of film but also enthusiastic creators who now, more than ever, are empowered by the accessibility of affordable equipment, free online resources such as editing software, and numerous free platforms for distribution and publicity.

Here are several key reasons why filmmaking holds immense appeal and accessibility for young adults:

1. Creative Expression: Filmmaking provides an unparalleled outlet for creative expression, allowing young adults to channel their ideas, emotions, and perspectives into visually compelling narratives. From writing scripts and developing characters to crafting visual compositions and editing sequences, every aspect of the filmmaking process offers opportunities for self-expression and artistic explo-

ration. Whether it's a personal story inspired by their own personal experiences or an imaginative fantasy world of their own creation, young filmmakers have the freedom to bring any creative visions to life on screen.

2. Technological Advancements: The rapid advancements in digital technology have democratized the filmmaking process, making high-quality equipment and software more accessible and affordable than ever before. With a smartphone or a consumer-grade camera and basic editing software that is now included free with most operating systems, anyone can shoot, edit, and produce near professional-looking films from the comfort of their own homes. Additionally, online tutorials through platforms like YouTube, forums, and communities provide valuable resources and support for aspiring filmmakers, helping them to develop their skills and navigate the intricacies of the filmmaking process.

3. Collaborative Opportunities: Filmmaking is inherently collaborative, requiring teamwork, communication, and cooperation among a diverse range of individuals with varying skills and talents. For young adults, collaborating on film projects offers valuable opportunities to connect with friends, build relationships, and learn from one another's strengths and perspectives. Whether working with friends, classmates in a visual arts programs (like mine at Red Bank Regional High School in New Jersey), or fellow members of a filmmaking club or community, young filmmakers can develop crucial interpersonal skills and cultivate a sense of togetherness and solidarity that extends beyond the confines of the screen.

A classmate and I collaborating
on a project in our film program

4. Social Impact: Film has the power to inspire, educate, and change people's viewpoints of the world, making it an effective tool for raising awareness about important social issues and sparking meaningful conversations among young adults. From documentaries that shed light on systematic issues or promote social change to narrative films that challenge stereotypes and promote empathy and understanding with underlying meanings, filmmaking allows young adults to engage with the world around them and make a positive impact through their storytelling.

5. Career Opportunities: Beyond its artistic and creative appeal, filmmaking also offers viable career opportunities for young adults with a passion for storytelling and visual communication. From traditional roles such as directors, producers, and cinematographers to rapidly developing fields like digital content creation, virtual reality, streaming platforms, and the business aspects of filmmaking (my preferred area of study), the film industry encompasses a wide range of career paths and opportunities for young professionals. By honing their skills and gaining practical experience through independent projects, internships, and networking opportunities, young filmmakers can pursue fulfilling careers in the dynamic and ever-evolving world of film and media.

Whether as a hobby, a passion project, or a professional pursuit, filmmaking empowers young adults to unleash their creativity, share their stories with the world, and make their mark on the vibrant and dynamic landscape of cinema.

Me portraying a "neighborhood informant kid" on NBC's "The Blacklist"

Me working on the set of an A24 film

Me (far right, blue shirt) portraying a "park kid"
in Paramount's "Clifford the Big Red Dog"

Me (far right, blue shirt) portraying a "park kid"
in Paramount's "Clifford the Big Red Dog"

Me, "punch-bowl kid" in
CBS's "God Friended Me"

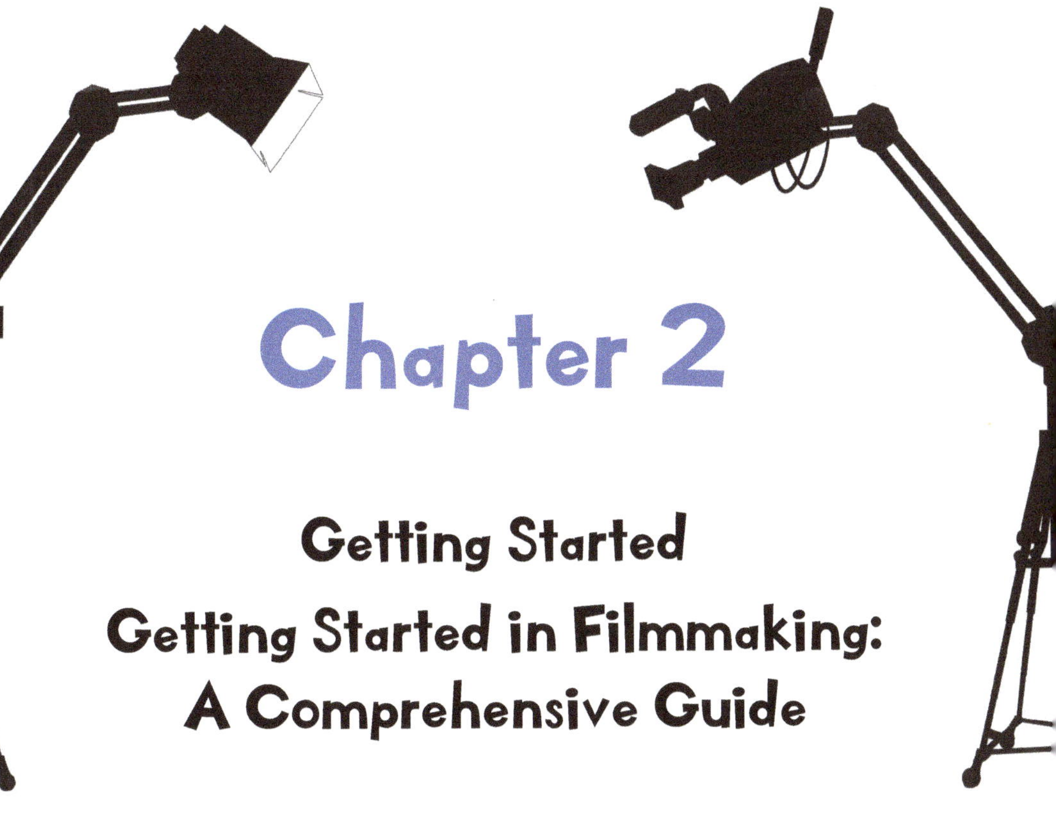

Chapter 2

Getting Started
Getting Started in Filmmaking: A Comprehensive Guide

Embarking on one's first journey into filmmaking is an exhilarating process that combines creativity, technical skill, and collaboration. Whether you're a novice filmmaker with a passion for storytelling or an experienced enthusiast looking to improve your skills, understanding the fundamentals is crucial for success. In this guide, I will explore the essential steps and considerations for getting started in filmmaking, touching on everything from storytelling and scriptwriting to equipment selection, team assembly, and finding that ever so elusive "inspiration."

A. Understanding the Basics: Storytelling, Scriptwriting, and Storyboarding

1. Storytelling: At the heart of every great film is a compelling story that captivates and resonates with audiences. Understanding the principles of storytelling is essential for creating engaging narratives that provoke emotion and thought, and leave a lasting impression. Whether you're exploring the depths of human drama, unraveling the mysteries of science fiction, or embarking on epic adventures, storytelling forms the foundation of your filmmaking journey.

   Key elements of storytelling include:

   - Character development: Creating multidimensional characters with distinct personalities, motivations, and "arcs" (a fancy phrase used in the industry). Characters that the audience cares about and can develop relationships with are arguably the most important element of a good storyline, and they are key in ensuring true engagement in a story.
   - Plot structure: Establishing a clear beginning, middle, and end, with well-defined conflicts, obstacles, and resolutions.
   - Theme exploration: Exploring universal themes and ideas that resonate with audiences on a personal and (hopefully) emotional level.

2. Scriptwriting: Once you've conceptualized your story, the next step is to translate it into a screenplay—a blueprint for your film that guides the entire production process.

Effective script writing requires a mastery of dialogue, pacing, and visual descriptions of what is in your "mind's eye" to effectively convey your story on the page. The magic of script writing and refinement was laid bare for me when I was fortunate enough to work with a well-known Hollywood writer (who had written the script for and was directing this particular film) during one of my summer breaks.

Key components of scriptwriting include:

- Dialogue: Crafting authentic dialogue that reflects the voices and personalities of your characters while advancing the plot.
- Scene description: Using words to paint vivid images with concise and evocative language in order to portray what exactly is occurring in a scene. I'll admit, this can be tough. These descriptions need to be carefully crafted and detailed enough to ensure that readers, other than yourself, can immerse themselves in the world of your story.
- Structure: Adhering to established screenplay formats and conventions, such as proper formatting, scene transitions, and page length. This can be thought of as the standard "rules" of scriptwriting.

3. Storyboarding: Storyboarding is the process of visually planning your film by creating a sequence of illustrated panels that represent each shot and scene. This invaluable tool allows you to visualize your story, plan camera angles, and establish pacing before filming begins. It can be thought of as a "comic/cartoon strip" summary of the

film's plot and storyline. It's also a very helpful organizational tool.

Key aspects of storyboarding include:

- Shot composition: Determining the framing, camera movement, and visual elements of each shot to effectively convey the desired mood and tone.
- Continuity: Ensuring consistency and coherence between shots to maintain a seamless narrative flow.
- Props/Items: Determining what physical items you need to prepare for usage when filming, both on and off screen.
- Collaboration: Collaborating with your cinematographer, director and production team to translate your vision from script to screen effectively.

B. Choosing the Right Equipment: Cameras, Lighting, and Sound

1. Cameras: Selecting the right camera is essential for capturing high-quality images that bring your story to life. With a wide range of options available (some more affordable than others), from professional cinema cameras to consumer-grade DSLRs and smartphones, choosing the best camera for your project depends on factors such as budget, technical requirements, and artistic preferences.

My current primary camera

Key considerations when choosing a camera include:

- Resolution: Determining the desired resolution—such as HD, 4K, or even higher—for your project based on delivery requirements, visual aesthetic, and post-production factors.
- Sensor size: Evaluating the sensor size and type—such as full-frame, APS-C, or Micro Four Thirds—and its impact on image quality, depth of field, and low-light performance.
- Features: Assessing additional features and capabilities, such as frame rates, dynamic range, and lens compatibility to meet your specific shooting needs.

2. Lighting: Lighting plays a crucial role in shaping the look and feel of your film, setting the mood, and highlighting key elements within the frame. Whether you're shooting indoors or outdoors, understanding the principles of lighting and mastering various techniques is essential for achieving professional results.

Key aspects of lighting for filmmaking include:

- Key light: The primary light source that illuminates the subject and establishes the overall lighting direction and intensity.
- Fill light: Supplementary light used to fill in shadows and balance the contrast between light and dark areas within the frame.
- Backlight: Accent light positioned behind the subject to create separation and depth, adding dimensionality to the image.

3. Sound: Sound is often referred to as the "invisible art" of filmmaking, as it plays a crucial role in enhancing the viewer's emotional engagement and immersion in the story. From dialogue and ambient noise to music and sound effects, achieving clear, high-quality sound requires careful planning and attention to detail. Poor sound, in my opinion, has a more negative impact than poor image.

Key considerations for capturing and recording sound include:

- Microphones: Choosing the right microphone—such as shotgun, lavalier, boom, etc.—to capture clear and natural-sounding audio in various shooting conditions.

- Location sound: Managing environmental factors, such as background noise, wind, and echoes, to ensure optimal sound quality during filming.
- Post-production: Editing and mixing sound elements—such as dialogue, music, and effects—in post-production to enhance clarity, balance, and overall impact.

C. Assembling Your Team: Roles and Responsibilities on a Film Set

1. Director: The director is the creative visionary behind the film, responsible for translating the script into a visual and emotional experience for the audience. Working closely with the cast and crew, the director oversees all aspects of production, from casting and rehearsals to blocking, shooting, and editing.

   Key responsibilities of the director include:

   - Conceptualizing the visual style and aesthetic of the film.
   - Collaborating with the cinematographer to plan camera angles, framing, and movement.
   - Directing the performances of the actors to achieve the desired emotional depth and authenticity.
   - On lower level projects, like student films, the role of director is often combined with the writer and producer, which entails additional responsibilities.

2. Producer: On larger scale projects, the producer(s) are equal with the director at the top of the hierarchy. While the director handles all creative aspects of the project, the producer oversees and coordinates the production process from start to finish and is a pivotal role in ensuring a high-quality finished product

    Key responsibilities of the producer include:

    - Organizing and securing ample funding for the project.
    - Collaborating with the director to put together the team and select crew members.
    - Budgeting and overseeing funds throughout production.
    - Ensuring that the project stays on schedule, and on track for completion in time.
    - Negotiating with distributors, exhibitors, and media companies to determine what type of release the film will get following completion.
    - Scheduling and organizing locations, facilities, cast and crew members, and props.
    - On lower- level projects, like student films, the role of producer is often combined with the writer and director, which entails additional responsibilities.

3. Cinematographer: The cinematographer, also known as the director of photography (DP), is responsible for capturing the visual essence of the film through the art of cinematography. Working closely with the director, the cinematographer translates the director's vision into compelling imagery using lighting, composition, and camera movement.

Key responsibilities of the cinematographer include:

- Working with the director to select the appropriate camera and lenses to achieve the desired look and feel of the film.
- Designing and executing lighting setups to enhance mood, atmosphere, and storytelling.
- Collaborating with the camera crew to capture dynamic and visually striking shots.
- Collaborating with editors in post-production to maintain the intended look and feel.

4. Editor: The editor plays a crucial role in shaping the narrative and pacing of the film through the art of editing. Working closely with the director, the editor assembles raw footage into a cohesive and compelling story, refining performances, cutting unnecessary scenes, and adding visual and sound effects to enhance the overall impact of the film.

Key responsibilities of the editor include:

- Organizing and cataloging raw footage into a manageable and efficient editing workflow.
- Crafting the structure and rhythm of the film through the arrangement of shots, scenes, and sequences.
- Collaborating with the director and sound designer to create a seamless and immersive audio-visual experience.
- Collaborating with the cinematographer to maintain the intended look and feel.

Finding inspiration is a fundamental aspect of the filmmaking process, and exploring different genres and styles is key to unlocking creativity and discovering one's unique voice as a filmmaker. Each genre offers its own set of conventions, themes, and storytelling techniques, providing filmmakers with a rich tapestry of possibilities to explore and interpret. Here, we delve deeper into the importance of exploring different genres and styles in filmmaking:

Broadening Horizons

Exploring different genres and styles exposes filmmakers to a diverse range of cinematic experiences, from the heart-pounding thrills of action-adventure to the thought-provoking depths of drama and the fantastical realms of science fiction and fantasy. By immersing themselves in a variety of genres, filmmakers gain a deeper appreciation for the breadth and depth of storytelling possibilities, expanding their horizons and challenging their creative boundaries.

Cultivating a Well-Rounded Skill Set

Great filmmakers are known for their versatility, as they are able to effectively work across different genres and styles. This adaptability is crucial for meeting the diverse demands of storytelling. Whether it's mastering the fast-paced editing of action films, delving into the nuanced emotions of character-driven dramas, or creating visually stunning fantasy epics, filmmakers who embrace variety become skilled at navigating the unique challenges and opportunities each genre offers.

Finding Personal Expression

When filmmakers explore various genres and styles, they often uncover aspects of themselves and their artistic sensibilities that strongly connect with their creative vision. Whether they are attracted to the emotional depth of romance, the ironic wit of satire, or the profound questions of existentialism, filmmakers express themselves through the narratives they decide to share and the themes they delve into. Through experimenting with diverse genres and styles, filmmakers reveal their individual voice and viewpoint, adding authenticity and depth to their work.

Pushing Creative Boundaries

Trying out various genres and styles inspires filmmakers to think outside the box and go beyond traditional storytelling conventions. By mixing different genres or defying audience expectations, filmmakers can produce fresh and surprising cinematic experiences that stimulate, challenge, and motivate. Whether they are playing with unconventional storytelling methods, unique visual approaches, or innovative narrative structures, filmmakers who push the boundaries open up new avenues and redefine the potential of cinema

Connecting with Audiences

Various genres and styles connect with varying audiences, showcasing different tastes, interests, and cultural viewpoints. Filmmakers can engage a wider audience and create stronger emotional bonds through storytelling by delving into a range of genres and styles. Understanding the specific charm of each genre allows filmmakers to tailor their work to better captivate audiences and evoke the desired emotions, whether it be laughter, tears, or suspense. In essence, exploring different genres and styles is a crucial part of the filmmaking process, providing filmmakers with endless possibilities for inspiration, development, and self-exploration. By expanding their horizons, honing their skills, and expressing their unique voice, filmmakers can truly connect with their audience on a deeper level.

In conclusion, exploring different genres and styles is an essential aspect of the filmmaking journey, offering filmmakers endless opportunities for inspiration, growth, and self-discovery. By broadening horizons, cultivating versatility, finding personal expression, pushing creative boundaries, and connecting with audiences, filmmakers who embrace a diverse range of genres and styles enrich their artistic practice and elevate the power of cinema to inspire, entertain, and enlighten audiences around the world.

Chapter 3

Production: Bringing Your Vision to Life

Production is the stage of filmmaking where the script comes alive, and the vision of the director begins to take shape on screen. It encompasses a multitude of tasks, from setting up shots and directing actors to managing the crew and capturing sound. In this chapter, we will delve into each aspect of production, exploring the intricacies of framing, composition, and camera movements, the art of directing actors, the importance of crew management, and the nuances of capturing sound.

A. Setting up Your Shots: Framing, Composition, and Camera Movements

1. Framing: Framing refers to the placement and arrangement of visual elements within the frame of the camera. It is a crucial aspect of cinematography that determines how

the audience perceives and interprets the action on screen. Different types of framing can evoke various emotions and convey different meanings, adding depth and dimension to the storytelling process.

Key techniques for framing include:

- Establishing shots: Wide shots that establish the setting and context of the scene.
- Close-ups: Tight shots that focus on a specific subject or detail, conveying intimacy and intensity.
- Rule of thirds: A compositional guideline that divides the frame into thirds horizontally and vertically, with key elements placed along the intersecting lines or at their intersections for balanced and visually pleasing compositions.
- Framing within framing: Using objects or architectural elements within the frame to frame the main subject, adding layers of visual interest and depth.

An example of framing in one of my own projects

2. Composition: Composition refers to the arrangement and organization of visual elements within the frame to create visually compelling images. It encompasses factors such as framing, camera angle, depth of field, and symmetry, all of which contribute to the overall aesthetic and impact of the shot.

    Key principles of composition include:

    - Balance: Distributing visual weight evenly across the frame to create a sense of harmony and equilibrium.
    - Leading lines: Using lines, such as roads, fences, or architectural features, to guide the viewer's eye toward the main subject or focal point of the shot.
    - Symmetry and asymmetry: Arranging visual elements symmetrically or asymmetrically within the frame to create a sense of order or tension, respectively.
    - Negative space: Using empty or negative space around the main subject to draw attention to it and create a sense of isolation or emphasis.

**Examples of shot composition
in some of my own projects.**

3. Camera Movements: Camera movements add dynamism and fluidity to the visual storytelling process, allowing filmmakers to convey movement, perspective, and emotion through the motion of the camera. Whether panning, tilting, tracking, or zooming, each camera movement serves a specific purpose and contributes to the overall narrative impact of the shot.

    Common camera movements include:

    - Pan: Horizontal movement of the camera from left to right or right to left, used to follow action or reveal new information within the frame.
    - Tilt: Vertical movement of the camera up or down, used to change perspective or emphasize vertical elements within the frame.
    - Tracking/dolly: Movement of the camera along a track or dolly, used to follow subjects or create smooth, fluid motion.
    - Zoom: Adjustment of the focal length of the lens to change the size of the subject within the frame, used to emphasize details or create a sense of intimacy or distance.

B. Directing Actors: Communication, Collaboration, and Bringing Characters to Life

1. Communication: Effective communication is the cornerstone of successful directing, enabling directors to articulate their vision, provide clear instructions, and collaborate with actors to achieve authentic and compelling performances. Building trust and rapport with actors is essential

for creating a collaborative and supportive working environment where creativity can flourish.

Key communication techniques include:

- Active listening: Paying attention to actors' concerns, ideas, and feedback, and incorporating their input into the creative process.
- Clear direction: Providing specific and actionable guidance to actors, such as emotional beats, character motivations, and blocking instructions, to help them understand and embody their roles.
- Empathy and understanding: Recognizing and validating actors' emotions and experiences, and creating a safe space for them to explore and express themselves authentically.

2. Collaboration: Directing actors is a collaborative process that requires mutual respect, trust, and a shared commitment to realizing the director's vision. By fostering a collaborative atmosphere on set, directors can harness the collective creativity and talent of their cast and crew, resulting in richer and more nuanced performances.

Key collaboration strategies include:

- Rehearsals: Conducting rehearsals with actors to explore character dynamics, refine performances, and experiment with blocking and staging before filming begins.
- Open dialogue: Encouraging actors to share their insights, ideas, and concerns, and actively solicit-

ing feedback from cast and crew members to foster a sense of ownership and investment in the project.

- Flexibility and adaptability: Remaining open to new ideas, improvisation, and creative experimentation, and embracing unexpected discoveries and opportunities that arise during the filming process.

3. Bringing Characters to Life: Directors play a pivotal role in bringing characters to life, guiding actors through the process of character development, emotional exploration, and performance enhancement. By understanding the nuances of character psychology, motivation, and behavior, directors can help actors embody their roles with depth, authenticity, and nuance.

Key techniques for bringing characters to life include:

- Character analysis: Collaborating with actors to analyze the motivations, desires, and conflicts of their characters, and develop a deeper understanding of their inner lives and emotional journeys.
- Emotional connection: Encouraging actors to draw on their own experiences, memories, and emotions to infuse their performances with authenticity, vulnerability, and relatability.
- Physicality and embodiment: Guiding actors in the exploration of physical gestures, mannerisms, and vocal inflections that reflect the unique personality and essence of their characters.

C. Managing the Crew: Delegating Tasks, Problem Solving, and Maintaining Morale

1. Delegating Tasks: Managing the crew involves delegating tasks and responsibilities to ensure that all aspects of production run smoothly and efficiently. From camera operators and lighting technicians to production assistants and grips, each member of the crew plays a vital role in bringing the director's vision to life.

   Key principles of task delegation include:

   - Clear roles and responsibilities: Establishing clear lines of communication and defining each crew member's role and responsibilities to avoid confusion and minimize duplication of effort.
   - Effective leadership: Providing guidance, support, and direction to crew members, and empowering them to take ownership of their tasks and contribute to the overall success of the production.
   - Flexibility and adaptability: Remaining flexible and adaptable in response to changing circumstances, unforeseen challenges, and evolving production needs, and adjusting task assignments accordingly to ensure that production stays on track.

2. Problem Solving: Production is inherently unpredictable, and unforeseen challenges and obstacles are bound to arise during filming. Effective crew management involves identifying problems, implementing solutions, and maintaining a positive and solution-oriented mindset to keep the production moving forward.

Key strategies for problem solving include:

- Anticipation and preparation: Anticipating potential problems and challenges before they arise, and proactively implementing contingency plans and mitigation strategies to minimize their impact on production.
- Collaboration and teamwork: Encouraging open communication, collaboration, and brainstorming among crew members to identify creative solutions and overcome obstacles together.
- Adaptability and resourcefulness: Remaining flexible and resourceful in the face of unexpected setbacks, and leveraging available resources, expertise, and ingenuity to find innovative solutions to problems as they arise.

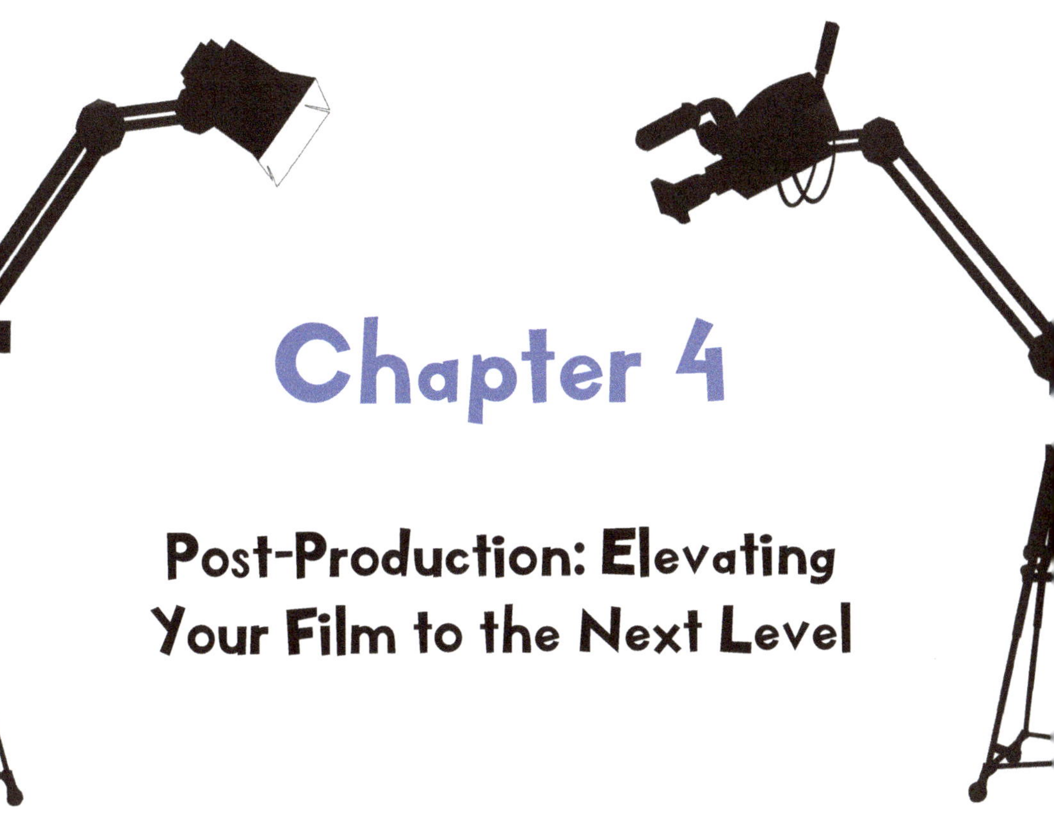

Chapter 4

Post-Production: Elevating Your Film to the Next Level

Post-production is the final stage of the filmmaking process, where raw footage is transformed into a polished and cohesive cinematic experience. From editing and enhancing visuals to polishing sound and adding final touches, post-production plays a crucial role in shaping the overall look, feel, and impact of a film. In this comprehensive guide, we'll explore each aspect of post-production, covering editing basics, visual enhancement, sound polishing, and final touches to prepare your film for distribution.

A. Editing Basics: Cutting, Pacing, and Adding Transitions

1. Cutting: Editing is the art of assembling raw footage into a coherent and engaging narrative. Cutting involves selecting the best takes, trimming excess footage, and arranging

scenes in a logical and compelling sequence. By cutting out unnecessary shots, tightening pacing, and maintaining continuity, editors create a seamless flow that keeps audiences engaged from the first frame to the last.

Key cutting techniques include:

- Removing distractions: Cutting out extraneous dialogue, action, or imagery that does not contribute to the story or character development.
- Establishing rhythm: Using cuts, transitions, and pacing to establish the rhythm and tempo of the film, creating tension, suspense, or emotional impact as needed.
- Maintaining continuity: Ensuring visual and narrative continuity between shots to create a seamless and immersive viewing experience.

2. Pacing: Pacing refers to the overall rhythm and tempo of a film, determined by the pacing of individual scenes, the length of shots, and the pacing of editing transitions. By controlling the pace of the film, editors can manipulate audience perception of time, build tension, and evoke emotional responses.

    Key pacing techniques include:

    - Varying shot length: Using a mix of short, medium, and long shots to create dynamic pacing and maintain audience engagement.
    - Enhancing transitions: Using editing techniques such as cuts, fades, and dissolves to smooth transitions between scenes and control the flow of time.
    - Leveraging sound design: Incorporating sound effects, music, and silence to enhance pacing and create mood and atmosphere.

3. Adding Transitions: Transitions are used to connect one shot or scene to another, providing visual cues to the audience and helping to establish the temporal and spatial relationship between scenes. From simple cuts to more elaborate transitions like fades, dissolves, and wipes, transitions can add texture, rhythm, and continuity to the editing process.

    Common types of transitions include:

    - Cut: A direct transition from one shot to another, creating a seamless and immediate visual connection between scenes.
    - Fade: A gradual transition from one shot to another, typically accompanied by a fade to black

or white, used to indicate a change in time, location, or mood.

- Dissolve: A gradual transition in which one shot fades out as another fades in, creating a smooth and seamless blend between scenes.

B. Enhancing Visuals: Color Grading, Visual Effects, and Graphics

1. Color Grading: Color grading is the process of adjusting and enhancing the color, contrast, and overall look of a film to achieve a desired aesthetic and mood. From subtle color corrections to bold stylistic choices, color grading can dramatically impact the visual tone and emotional resonance of a film.

   Key aspects of color grading include:

   - Color balance: Adjusting the balance of primary colors—red, green, and blue—to achieve natural-looking skin tones and overall color harmony.
   - Contrast and exposure: Enhancing contrast and adjusting exposure levels to create depth, dimension, and visual impact.
   - Creative grading: Applying creative color grading techniques, such as stylized looks, film emulations, and color filters, to enhance mood and atmosphere and evoke specific emotional responses.

2. Visual Effects: Visual effects (VFX) are computer-generated imagery (CGI) or practical effects used to create or enhance elements that cannot be captured during production. From adding fantastical creatures and environments

to enhancing practical effects and creating seamless composites, VFX allows filmmakers to realize their creative vision and push the boundaries of storytelling.

Key categories of visual effects include:

- CGI: Computer-generated imagery used to create realistic or fantastical elements, such as creatures, characters, environments, and special effects.
- Matte painting: Hand-painted or digitally created backgrounds used to extend or enhance practical sets and locations, adding depth and detail to the visual landscape.
- Motion graphics: Animated graphics and typography used to convey information, enhance storytelling, and create visual interest in titles, credits, and other on-screen elements.

3. Graphics: Graphics are used to convey information, identify characters, and enhance storytelling through visual elements such as titles, credits, and on-screen text. Whether designing elaborate title sequences or creating subtle lower thirds, graphics play a crucial role in shaping the overall aesthetic and narrative flow of a film.

Common types of graphics include:

- Titles: On-screen text used to introduce the film, identify key cast and crew members, and convey other pertinent information to the audience.
- Credits: End credits that list the cast, crew, and other contributors to the film, typically accompanied by music or other audio cues.

- Lower thirds: On-screen graphics that identify characters, locations, or other contextual information, typically displayed in the lower third of the frame during interviews or documentary-style segments.

C. Polishing the Sound: Mixing

1. Mixing: Sound mixing is the process of combining and balancing multiple audio elements—such as dialogue, music, sound effects, and ambient noise—to create a cohesive and immersive sonic experience. By adjusting volume levels, spatial placement, and frequency balance, sound mixers enhance clarity, depth, and impact to ensure that every sound serves the overall narrative and emotional tone of the film.

   Key aspects of sound mixing include:

   - Dialogue clarity: Ensuring that dialogue remains clear and intelligible amidst other audio elements, such as music, sound effects, and ambient noise.
   - Spatial positioning: Using stereo and surround sound techniques to create a sense of space and dimensionality, immersing viewers in the world of the film and enhancing their emotional engagement.
   - Dynamic range: Balancing the dynamic range of audio elements to maintain consistency and prevent distortion, ensuring that quiet moments are audible and loud moments are impactful.

D. Final Touches: Adding Titles, Credits, and Preparing for Distribution

1. Adding Titles and Credits: Titles and credits are essential elements of any film, providing important information about the cast, crew, and production team while also setting the tone for the viewing experience. From the opening titles that introduce the film to the closing credits that acknowledge the contributions of everyone involved, adding titles and credits is a critical step in the post-production process.

   Key considerations for adding titles and credits include:

   - Title design: Designing visually engaging and thematically appropriate title sequences that reflect the style and tone of the film.
   - Font selection: Choosing appropriate fonts for titles and credits that are legible, aesthetically pleasing, and consistent with the overall design of the film.
   - Timing and placement: Timing the appearance of titles and credits to coincide with key moments in the film, such as character introductions or significant plot developments, and placing them in locations that do not detract from the on-screen action.
   - Credits hierarchy: Organizing credits in a hierarchical manner, with key creative and production personnel listed first, followed by supporting cast and crew members, and concluding with special thanks and acknowledgments.

2. Preparing for Distribution: Preparing a film for distribution involves finalizing technical aspects, ensuring compatibility with distribution platforms, and complying with industry standards and regulations. Whether distributing a film theatrically, digitally, or on physical media, proper preparation is essential to ensure that the film reaches its intended audience in the best possible quality.

Key steps in preparing for distribution include:

- Technical specifications: Adhering to technical specifications for resolution, aspect ratio, frame rate, and audio format required by distribution platforms and delivery formats.
- Quality control: Conducting thorough quality control checks to identify and address any technical issues or errors, such as audio sync problems, visual artifacts, or encoding errors.
- Metadata and artwork: Providing accurate metadata, such as title, synopsis, genre, and cast and crew information, along with high-quality artwork, such as posters and promotional images, to accompany the film during distribution.
- Delivery formats: Generating delivery formats compatible with distribution platforms and audience preferences, such as digital files for streaming services, DCP (Digital Cinema Package) for theatrical distribution, and Blu-ray or DVD for physical media distribution.
- Rights management: Securing necessary legal rights and clearances for music, images, and other copyrighted material used in the film, and obtain-

ing appropriate licenses and permissions for distribution in different territories and formats.

Adding titles, credits, and preparing for distribution are crucial final touches that complete the post-production process and prepare a film for release to audiences worldwide. By carefully designing titles and credits that complement the film's aesthetic and narrative, and ensuring that the film meets technical specifications and regulatory requirements for distribution, filmmakers can maximize the impact and reach of their work, bringing their vision to life on screens big and small.

Chapter 5

Sharing Your Film

A. Film Festivals: Submitting Your Work, Networking, and Gaining Exposure

Film festivals offer filmmakers an invaluable opportunity to showcase their work, connect with industry professionals, and gain exposure to diverse audiences. Submitting your film to festivals requires careful planning and strategy to maximize your chances of acceptance and make the most of the festival experience.

Key considerations for navigating film festivals include:

- Researching festivals: Identifying festivals that align with your film's genre, style, and target audience, and researching their submission guidelines, selection criteria, and deadlines.
- Crafting a compelling submission: Preparing a polished submission package that includes a high-quality screener, engaging synopsis, filmmaker bio, and any additional materials required by the festival.

- Networking and promotion: Attending festival events, screenings, and networking sessions to connect with fellow filmmakers, industry professionals, and potential collaborators, and actively promoting your film through social media, press releases, and word-of-mouth.
- Maximizing exposure: Leveraging festival screenings, awards, and accolades to generate buzz and attract attention from distributors, sales agents, and media outlets, and capitalizing on opportunities for press coverage, reviews, and interviews.

B. Online Platforms: Uploading to YouTube, Vimeo, and Social Media

In today's digital age, online platforms offer filmmakers a powerful and accessible way to share their work with global audiences, bypassing traditional distribution channels and reaching viewers directly. Uploading your film to platforms such as YouTube, Vimeo, and social media sites can provide instant exposure and enable you to connect with viewers around the world.

Key strategies for leveraging online platforms include:

- Choosing the right platform: Selecting the platform that best suits your film's goals, whether it's reaching a wide audience on YouTube, showcasing your work in high quality on Vimeo, or engaging with fans on social media platforms like Facebook, Instagram, and Twitter.
- Optimizing your content: Optimizing your film's title, description, tags, and thumbnail to improve visibility and searchability on online platforms, and leveraging features such as annotations, end screens, and hashtags to encourage engagement and interaction with viewers.

- Engaging with your audience: Responding to comments, messages, and feedback from viewers, and actively promoting your film through social media posts, updates, and shares to build a loyal fanbase and cultivate a community around your work.

- Monetization and distribution: Exploring opportunities for monetization through advertising, sponsorship, merchandise sales, and crowdfunding, and considering distribution options, such as streaming services, video-on-demand platforms, and online marketplaces to reach new audiences and generate revenue.

C. Screening Events: Organizing Premieres, Q&A Sessions, and Community Screenings

Screening events provide filmmakers with a unique opportunity to engage directly with audiences, share insights into their creative process, and foster meaningful connections with supporters and fans. Whether organizing a premiere, hosting a Q&A session, or organizing a community screening, planning and executing successful events requires careful coordination and attention to detail.

Key steps for organizing screening events include:

- Selecting venues: Choosing venues that are appropriate for the size and scale of your event, whether it's a traditional theater, art house cinema, community center, or outdoor screening venue, and securing necessary permits, licenses, and insurance.

- Promoting your event: Creating eye-catching promotional materials, such as posters, flyers, and digital ads, to generate excitement and anticipation for your screening, and leveraging social media, email newsletters, and local press to reach potential attendees and build attendance.

- Planning logistics: Coordinating logistics such as ticketing, seating, concessions, and technical setup, and ensuring that all aspects of the event run smoothly and professionally to create a positive experience for attendees.

- Engaging your audience: Hosting engaging post-screening Q&A sessions, panel discussions, or meet-and-greet opportunities with cast and crew members to provide insights into the filmmaking process, answer questions from the audience, and foster a sense of community and connection around your film.

D. Feedback and Reflection: Learning from Criticism, Celebrating Achievements, and Planning Your Next Project

Feedback and reflection are essential aspects of the filmmaking process, providing opportunities for growth, learning, and self-improvement. Whether receiving constructive criticism from audiences and peers, celebrating achievements and milestones, or reflecting on lessons learned and planning for the future, embracing feedback and reflection can help filmmakers evolve and evolve their craft.

Key strategies for feedback and reflection include:

- Seeking constructive criticism: Soliciting feedback from audiences, peers, mentors, and industry professionals through screenings, festivals, online reviews, and workshops, and approaching criticism with an open mind and a willingness to learn and improve.

- Celebrating achievements: Acknowledging and celebrating the achievements and milestones of your film, whether it's winning awards, receiving positive reviews, or reaching significant audience milestones, and taking time to appreciate the hard work and dedication that went into bringing your vision to life.

- Reflecting on lessons learned: Reflecting on the successes and challenges of your filmmaking journey, identifying areas for improvement, and extracting valuable lessons and insights that can inform your future projects and creative endeavors.

- Planning your next project: Using feedback and reflection to inform the development of your next project, whether it's refining your storytelling techniques, expanding your technical skills, or exploring new genres and styles, and approaching each new project with renewed enthusiasm, creativity, and purpose.

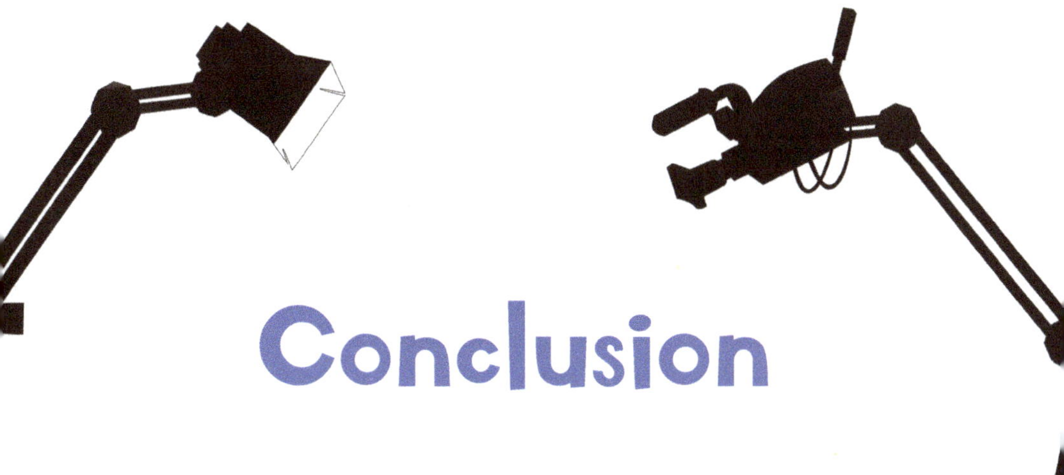

Conclusion

Pursue your passion!!

As we conclude this comprehensive guide to filmmaking, it's important to offer words of encouragement to young filmmakers embarking on their creative journey. Filmmaking is a challenging yet immensely rewarding pursuit that requires dedication, perseverance, and a willingness to learn and grow. While the road may be long and fraught with obstacles, it is also filled with endless opportunities for discovery, creativity, and self-expression.

To all aspiring filmmakers, I urge you to pursue your passion with courage and conviction. Embrace the joy of storytelling and the thrill of bringing your vision to life on screen. Remember that every film you create, whether big or small, represents a stepping stone on your path to mastery and success.

Never underestimate the power of continued learning and growth. Seek out opportunities to expand your knowledge, hone your skills, and collaborate with fellow filmmakers. Whether through formal education, hands-on experience, or mentorship from industry professionals, every lesson learned and every challenge overcome brings you one step closer to realizing your full potential as a filmmaker.

Above all, remember to stay true to yourself and your creative vision. Your unique voice and perspective are what make your films truly special. Embrace your strengths, celebrate your successes, and learn from your failures. And always remember that the most important part of filmmaking is not the destination, but the journey itself—the people you meet, the stories you tell, and the impact you make along the way.

So, to all the young filmmakers out there, I say: Keep dreaming, keep creating, and never stop reaching for the stars. The world of filmmaking is yours for the taking, and with passion, perseverance, and a dash of creativity, there's no limit to what you can achieve.

About
the Author

Stephen F. Canino is a young filmmaker with a lifelong passion for the craft, having embarked on his cinematic journey at the tender age of four. Actively involved in his local film community and a dedicated member of a renowned high school film program, Stephen's expertise, and enthusiasm shine through in his insightful guide for aspiring filmmakers. Before that, his early fascination with cameras and storytelling laid the foundation for his remarkable journey. Praised by mentors and peers alike for his talent and dedication, Stephen is a rising star in the world of independent filmmaking.